Seven Ways
Your God-Given Purpose
May Be Revealed

Seven Ways Your God-Given Purpose May Be Revealed

A Call to Christian Service

By
CLIFFORD A. PARKER

A division of Squire Publishers, Inc.
4500 College Blvd.
Leawood, KS 66211
1/888/888-7696

ISBN: 1-58597-168-5

Library of Congress Control Number: 2003101381

A division of Squire Publishers, Inc.
4500 College Blvd.
Leawood, KS 66211
1/888/888-7696

Contents

Introduction

Throughout my years of Christian ministry I have crossed the paths of many believers who have said, "God is keeping me alive for some reason," or "I know that God has a purpose for my life, but I really don't know what it is." This book is written to help those and thousands of other individuals gain knowledge on biblically and spiritually revealed ways God may use to make our life's purpose known to us. It is a wonderful feeling to know that God has a glorious and powerful purpose for each of us individually. It makes me feel special and individually loved and valued in the Kingdom of God. Each of our purpose is like a piece of a puzzle in the big picture of God's plan for man. God the Father is calling every man, woman, boy, and girl to fulfill the glorious purpose He has created us to serve.

Each of us will travel different roads at different times in our lives, crossing the paths of many souls. No one else will ever travel the same roads, cross the paths of the same individuals, at the same time, under the same condition and spiritual opportunities as you and I will individually. It is God's will to use us in ministry to touch the lives of many souls that cross our paths. No one else can fulfill our ministry purpose for us, we are individually accountable.

Every calling and purpose of God for man is good and powerful, both for man himself and for the Kingdom of God. As you seek to know God's purpose for your life, it is important to believe the Word of God and have a personal relationship with the Father, Son, and the Holy Spirit. The Holy Spirit is the divine Spirit of Christ sent to lead, guide, and empower each of us to do God's will. The scripture says in 1 Corinthians 2:11b, "... Even so no one knows the things of God except the Spirit of God" (The New King James Bible).

Human reasoning based on the wisdom of man can become a stumbling block to understanding spiritual revelations from Jesus Christ. As you read this book, I pray that God will bless you to be open to believe His words and receive from the Holy Spirit.

Read it prayerfully and listen to the voice of God as he speaks to your heart. Remember, your purpose in the service of Jesus Christ is first and foremost personal, between you and Christ only, then interconnects with the church of Jesus Christ universally.

1

God Has A Purpose For Each Life

"All things work together for good to those who love the lord and are called according to His purpose for them."

(Roman 8:28 New Living Translation)

God spoke to me in a dream on October 3, 1998 and told me to tell people everywhere that He has a purpose for every living soul and that each of our purpose can only be fulfilled in and through Jesus Christ. This book is written to communicate that message along with additional biblical and spiritual enlightenment that has been spiritually revealed to me on different ways God may use to reveal His purpose to us. I pray that after reading this book you will be moved in the Spirit to share this message with others.

Our Purpose Is Our Work In Ministry

Our God-given purpose is the work Christ has chosen, ordained, and called each of us to do in ministry.

Ministry means to be in Christian service (helping others) for the Lord Jesus Christ. Christ has ordained different ministries and different levels of ministries that He has chosen and called each of us to serve. The scriptures say in 1 Corinthians 12:5-6, *"And there are differences of ministries, but the same Lord. And there are diversities of activities, but it is the same God who works all in all"* (The New King James Bible). Fulfilling our God-called purposes takes us from glory to glory (one spiritual level to another) in our walk with Jesus Christ.

Three Great Christian Callings

The Bible teaches of three great spiritual callings upon our lives. First, we are called out of darkness, from sin to salvation (1 Peter 2:9). Secondly, we are called to holiness, righteous living (1 Peter 1:15-16). And thirdly, we are called to spiritual service, which is our vocation or work in ministry (Ephesians 4:1 and Roman 12:4). This book focuses on our call to service.

Callings / Expectations / Sanctification

Spiritual Callings	Expectations	Sanctification
➢Out of Darkness	→Believe/Accept/Confess	→Positional
➢To Holiness	→Righteous Living	→Progressive
➢To Purpose	→Ministry	→Service

Figure 1.1

2

Christian service reaches out beyond ourselves; it is carrying out our God-given duties to worship the Father and minister to the needs of our fellowman in Jesus' name. Every born again believer is required to be in Christian service; it is our individual purpose in ministry.

When we live the purpose God has for our lives, the emptiness, the lack of fulfillment, and the broken pieces of our lives and the lives of those Christ allows us to touch will begin to fall in place according to God's will for us. The Apostle Paul writes in his epistle to the Romans: *"All things work together for good to those who love the lord and are called according to His purpose for them"* (Roman 8:28 New Living Translation). Christ can and wants to do more with and for our lives than we can ever do for ourselves. Jesus says in His words, *"… I have come that they may have life, and that they may have it more abundantly."* (John 10:10 – New Living Translation). Living apart from the purpose of God, who created us, can cause many unnecessary struggles, heartaches, and problems, as well as cause us to come short of fulfilling God's eternal plans for our lives.

In our call to Christian service, believers have a commission, given certain authorities to carry out our commission, and are accountable to our divine Creator for fulfilling our commission.

Our Commission, Authority and Accountability

I have chosen three passages for scriptural references as a foundation on which to build this book. These passages speak to our ministry commission, our authority and power to carry out our commission, and the coming day of accountability. These passages continue to speak with power to my spirit; I hope they will speak to yours as well.

OUR COMMISSION

Matthew 28:18-20

18 *And Jesus came and spoke to them saying, "All authority has been given to Me in heaven and on earth."*

19 *"Go therefore and make disciples of all the nations, baptizing them in the name of the Father and of the Son and of the Holy Spirit.*

20 *"Teaching them to observe all things whatever I have commanded you; and behold, I am with you always, even to the end of the age." Amen.*

OUR POWER AND AUTHORITY

Acts 1:8

8 *"But you will receive power when the Holy Spirit has come upon you; and you will be witnesses to Me in Jerusalem, and in all Judea and Samaria, and to the end of the earth."*

Luke 10:19 –20

19 *"Behold, I give you authority to trample on serpents and scorpions, and over all the power of the enemy, and nothing shall by any means hurt you.*

20 *"Nevertheless do not rejoice in this, that the spirits are subject to you, but rather rejoice because your names are written in heaven."*

OUR ACCOUNTABILITY

Matthew 25:31-40

31 *"When the Son of Man comes in His glory, and all the holy angels with Him, then He will sit on the throne of His glory.*

32 *"And all the nations will be gathered before Him, and He will separate them one from another, as a shepherd divides his sheep from the goats.*

33 *"And He will set the sheep on His right hand, but the goats on the left.*

34 *"Then the King will say to those on His right hand, 'Come, you blessed of My Father, inherit the kingdom prepared for you from the foundation of the world:*

35 *'for I was hungry and you gave Me drink; I was a stranger and you took Me in;*

36 *'I was naked and you clothed me; I was sick and you visited Me; I was in prison and you came to Me.'*

37 *"Then the righteous will answer Him saying, 'Lord,*

**when did we see You hungry and feed You, or thirsty
and give You drink?**

38 **'Or when did we see You a stranger and take You
in, or naked and clothe You?**

39 **"Or when did we see You sick, or in prison, and
came to see You?'**

40 **"And the King will answer and say to them, Assuredly, I say to you, inasmuch as you have done it to
one of the least of these My brethren, you have done
it to Me."**

The ministry of Jesus Christ is awesome and powerful and is available to the whole world. As I read and
understand Ephesians 4:11-12, every saint is to be
equipped for the work of ministry. The essence of ministry is to share and demonstrate the love of God to the
world, through Jesus Christ our Lord.

God Wants to Show Himself Mightily In and Through Us

Christ's purpose for us in ministry is not based on
our qualifications, our financial position, nor formal
education. It is based on His will and power to show
Himself mightily in and through us. In other words,
rather than doing the things we feel capable of or have a
desire to do for Christ, we become vessels for Christ to
do his work in and through us, His way and in His time.

During my early years serving God's purpose as a

pastor, there were times when I thought that my biblical knowledge and educational achievements qualified me to minister. But my years of Christian growing pains have taught me that "*without Me (God) I can do nothing*" (John 15:5). God was merciful to me and blessed me to be successful, even with my pastoral weaknesses. He never let me down. But my limited understanding and trying to do spiritual things in my own wisdom and abilities have caused me to limit God's power working in me. I have since come to realize and now confess that I am a servant of God ministering His purpose for my life under the Spirit's direction and power.

Some individuals may feel that because of the lifestyles they have lived they are not worthy or qualified to minister with Christ. The fact is, none of us qualify within ourselves to minister with the King of Kings and Lord of Lords. It is only because of the love of God, demonstrated through Jesus Christ, that we are blessed to be used in ministry for and with Him. The Apostle Paul speaking to Timothy reminding him that their ministries were called and ordained by God says:

2 Timothy 1:8-9

8 *Therefore do not be ashamed of the testimony of our Lord, nor of me His prisoner, but share with me in the suffering for the gospel according to the power of God,*

9 *Who has saved us and called us with a holy call-*

ing, not according to our works, but according to His own purpose and grace which was given to us in Christ Jesus before time began.

General Versus *Individual* Purpose

As stated in the introduction, I have had the opportunity to meet and speak with many people concerning the purpose God has for their lives. Many have confessed that they know that God has a purpose for their lives, but most did not know what it is or was at the time. In most cases many would refer to our work in what I call g*eneral purpose. General purpose* is a ministry of holiness that God requires of all men, which includes loving God and man, providing for our families and caring for and nurturing our children in love. It also includes worshipping, praying, studying our Bibles, paying our bills, transforming our thought lives and conversations, yielding our bodies to God's glory, and walking as children of light. Romans 12:1-2 says it best, **"I beseech you therefore, brethren, by the mercies of God, that you present your bodies a living sacrifice, holy, acceptable to God, which is your reasonable service. And do not be conformed to this world, but be transformed by the renewing of your mind, that you may prove what is that good and acceptable and perfect will of God."** (The New King James Bible)

Our *individual purpose* is the calling Christ has upon each of our lives to serve him in a special way.

Commonly identifiable *individual purpose*s (ministering in our God-ordained work) include but not limited to church leadership ministries such as: preaching, teaching, being a pastor, priest, bishop, evangelist, prophet, and other ministries presented in this book.

The emphasis and focus of this book is to provide knowledge on the many other areas of Christian ministry that believers are called to serve in their God-ordained purpose. Ministering the gospel in the local church congregation is essential and is ordained by Jesus Christ, but keep in mind the great commission of taking the gospel to *"all the world."* One of the aims of this book is to identify the great need for ministers in the daily lives of people all over the world, in addition to the local church leadership and worship ministries.

Ministering Beyond the Local Church

Our *individual purposes* should be lived to worship God and serve others, to teach and demonstrate the truths of the gospel of Jesus Christ wherever the Spirit of Christ may lead us. The scripture says in 1 Corinthians 12:18, *" But now God has set the members, each one of them, in the body as it pleases him."*

Our individual purpose may be focused on families, areas of our neighborhood, hospitals, schools, among street people, political arena, ball courts and ball fields, judicial systems, factories, offices, clinics, laboratories, studios, supermarkets, shopping malls, airports, among sanitation workers and janitorial workers. Our *individual* ministry purpose may lead us to foreign lands, among the poor, the rich, the joyful, the sad, among the sick, the hungry, the elderly, the young, the runaways, drug addicts, prostitutes, the uneducated, the intellectuals, sometimes right where we are. I am not referring to a temporary evangelistic or witnessing seminar, I'm referring to a life journey or career in Christian service, touching the lives of others, as given to us by Jesus Christ.

Again, serving God in the area of our purpose does not mean that we should pull away from the local church. We are to continue to be a part of the local church and, in addition, live our God-given ministries in Christ inside and outside of the local church building, as led by the Holy Spirit. The scripture says, *"We are laborers together with God."* When our individual ministries and purposes are properly served, men, women, boys, and girls will be drawn to the local church for continual spiritual growth, worship, and fellowship with other believers.

God Makes His Purpose Known

Many people have left homes and families and have traveled to foreign lands in search of their purpose. One can only find his or her true purpose in God through Jesus Christ, our Creator and Redeemer. He is always with us knocking at the door of our hearts.

Throughout history God has revealed His purpose to man. Beginning in the Garden of Eden, God gave

Adam and Eve their purpose to *"Be fruitful and multiply; fill the earth and subdue it; have dominion over ...every living thing that moves on the earth."* (Genesis 1:28). The patriot Abraham was given the purpose by God to be the *"Father of many nations."* Genesis 17:4.

David was an anointed military leader, statesman, and king. Solomon was an anointed king, economist, and builder. God told the prophet Jeremiah, *"Before I formed you in the womb; Before you were born I sanctified you; And I ordained you a prophet to the nations."* Queen Esther had a God-given purpose to be married to King Xerxes to save the Jews from annihilation (Esther 4:14-16). The apostle Paul writing to Timothy said, *"Christ ordained us for this work even before the foundation of the world."* 2 Timothy 1:8-9. Jesus Himself said, *"I came not to do my own will but the will of Him who sent me."* Jesus' purpose was to "seek and save that which is lost."

The scriptures speaking to us in Proverbs 3:5-6 say, *"Trust in the Lord with all your heart and lean not on your own understanding; In all your ways acknowledge Him and He shall direct your paths."* Christ wants to direct each of our paths in ministry in ways that please and glorify Him. He is equipping each of us as ministers to reach souls for Him in every area of man's earthly existence.

2

Ways Our Individual Purpose May Be Revealed

"And there are differences of ministries, but the same Lord. And there are diversities of activities, but it is the same God who works all in all."

1 Cor. 12:5-6

Prior to December 1999, I was unclear on God's will to use everyone and anyone in ministry. I had been praying for some time for guidance on the subject. It wore so heavily on my heart that I wrote a research paper on the subject, after studying the views on ministry from other theologians. But still in my heart I needed to hear from God. Have you had times in your life when you wanted Christian counsel on a particular subject or matter and you sought advice from someone you believed would give you godly counsel? But after hearing the advice of your trusted spiritual advisor you still needed to hear from God Himself? That was my dilemma; I still needed to hear from God Himself. I'm thankful that God revealed His will to me on the subject. I am now convinced, without a doubt, that God can and will use anyone He desires to use in any area of ministry He wants him or her to serve.

As you read the various ways, discussed in this book, that Christ may choose to reveal his purpose for our lives listen to your heart and the voice of the Holy Spirit. Remember, your calling in ministry is first and foremost personal. Try to hear or recall times when God may have been revealing His purpose to you.

The seven ways are:
1. God may speak to us directly.
2. We may ask God in prayer to reveal His purpose to us.
3. Gifts of the Holy Spirit are given to help us fulfill our God-given purposes.
4. God uses visions and dreams to communicate His will and directions to us.
5. God may place a spiritual will or desire within our hearts.
6. God may provide frequent opportunities for us to serve in a particular area, evidenced by His anointing.
7. God may anoint a talent or ability for ministry.

No. 1 — God May Speak To Us Directly

"However, when He, the Spirit of truth, has come, He will guide you into all truth; for He will not speak on His own authority, but whatever He hears He will speak; and He will tell you things to come." — John 16:13

God speaks to us at different times and in different ways. He may speak to us in an audible voice, He may speak to our thought voice (mind), He may speak to our spirit man (heart), or He may speak to us through the holy scriptures. When God speaks to us in an audible voice, it may sound as if someone is in our presence speaking to us. We may actually hear the voice of God calling our names. If other people are in the general area as God speaks to us they will not hear the voice of God unless God intends for them to.

During the Christmas holiday season of 1997 my wife, daughter, and I, along with my brother's fiancée, were on an airplane flying from Newark, New Jersey to St. Louis, Missouri. We were on our way to Wichita, Kansas. My wife, daughter, and future sister-in-law were in the three seats immediately behind me. I was reading a spiritual helps book that my brother Isiah had given me while we were in New Jersey. About midway the flight I heard the voice of Christ speaking to me. Christ's voice was so clear and powerful that it startled me, I

SERVE IN
MY NAME

HEARING THE VOICE OF GOD

jumped in my seat.

I looked around through the corners of my eyes to see if anyone had seen me jump. I noticed my wife leaning forward, looking at me as if to say, "What's going on." It was during that conversation with the Lord when He told me that He wanted to use my wife in ministry. I said, "Lord, if you don't mind me asking, what do you want her to do?" The Lord's reply to me was, "To minister." In an instant I had a knowing in my spirit that the Lord was saying "to preach, teach, counsel, pray for, and lead my people in worship and righteousness."

One thing I have learned about talking with God in the Spirit, and that is, God may speak a few words that may take me a book of words to communicate and/or explain.

During my conversation with the Lord Jesus at 35,000 feet in the air, I gave Him the utmost reverence and respect. I was almost shaking in my seat during the whole conversation.

The first Saturday after landing in Wichita, Kansas, I moderated our church's yearly planning meeting. During the meeting I shared with the congregation what Christ told me during our flight. I also shared with the church that from that moment forward, in obedience to Christ, women would be free to preach the gospel in that church.

During that very meeting my wife and my wife's sister came forward to confess their call to the evangelistic ministry. They both stated that the Lord had spoken to them years before concerning their work in ministry, but they respected me as pastor and were waiting on Christ to change my heart before they stepped forward in their evangelistic calling. I now know that we can become stumbling blocks or hindrances to others in fulfilling their God-called purpose. I can now say in the words of Bishop T.D. Jakes, "Woman, thou art loosed."

God has spoken to many prophets of old in an audible voice. Moses heard the voice of God in an audible way as he turned to see a burning bush that would not be consumed. As a child God spoke to Jeremiah concerning his purpose in ministry.

Jeremiah wrote in chapter 1 verse 4-8: ***"The word of the Lord came to me, saying 'Before I formed you in the womb I knew you, before you were born I set you apart; I appointed you as a prophet to the nations. Ah, Sovereign Lord, I said, I do not know how to speak; I am only a child. But the Lord said to me, 'Do not say, I am only a child. You must go to everyone I send you to and say whatever I command you. Do not be afraid of them, for I am with you and will rescue you,' declares the Lord."***

God has spoken directly to prophets, through prophets, and angels during the Old Testament period to reveal His will for nations and tribes as well as for families and individuals. As a child the prophet Samuel heard the voice of God twice before the priest Eli realized who it was that was calling him. Eli told young Samuel that it was the voice of God and to answer Him the next time He called. The voice of God came to prophets such as Elijah, Elisha, Ezekiel, Hosea, Joel, Jonah and others.

God has also spoken to New Testament apostles such as the Apostle Paul and the Apostle Peter, giving them guidance in ministry. There were occasions when God the Father spoke to His Son Jesus Christ in an audible tone that others might hear Him.

The Thought Voice of God

Christ has spoken to me many times by his Spirit as a voice in my thoughts or mind. During those times I heard the voice of God just as loud and clear as if the sound waves had come through my outer ear.

I was blessed by God to successfully plant a new church in Wichita, Kansas. It is a small congregation and I was used by God to do much of the work around the church. During our early years of church growth I was the transportation driver, taught Sunday School, took care of the church grounds, taught Bible Study, church treasurer, sang in the choir, and ministered to the people.

At that time the church did not have a pianist, so I took piano lessons to help the church in that area. I spent many long hours practicing the piano to be of some help in the worship. I remember several Saturdays while at church practicing the piano I would hear the voice of Christ in my thoughts telling me to get off of the piano and get into the word of God. I would start reasoning in my mind that it was probably my own thoughts rather than the Spirit of God, so I foolishly continued to practice. I said foolishly because when the Spirit of God speaks to us it is important that we act on His will immediately, by faith. I allowed the voice of my own theological intellect to influence my actions. I thought practicing the piano to help the church in worship was a good thing. Have you ever tried to out-reason the thought voice of the Holy Spirit? That's just what Satan wants us to do.

Anyway, two or three weeks later I was at the church praying, asking God for guidance prior to my regular piano practice time. The voice of God came to me strong, clear, and powerful in my thoughts just as if someone was standing next to me speaking to me. The Spirit said to me, "Get off of the piano and get into My Word." That time the Spirit of God got my attention; I stopped practicing the piano and enrolled in a graduate level Christian Ministry degree program. I now realize that I needed further growth in my knowledge and understanding of the word of God to embark upon this teaching and publishing ministry. God was preparing me for this ministry before He revealed it to me.

A Still, Small Voice

God may also speak to our hearts or spirit man in a "still small voice." Elijah, an Old Testament prophet of

God, while he was hiding in the mountains, in a cave, as he was running from Jezebel, heard the still small voice of God.

1 Kings 19:11-15 (KJV)

11 *Then he said, "Go out, and stand on the mountain before the Lord.' And behold, the Lord passed by, and a great and strong wind tore into the mountains and broke the rocks in pieces before the Lord, but the Lord was not in the wind; and after the wind an earthquake, but the Lord was not in the earthquake;*

12 *and after the earthquake a fire, but the Lord was not in the fire; and after the fire a still small voice.*

13 *So it was, when Elijah heard it, that he wrapped his face in his mantle and went out and stood in the entrance of the cave. And suddenly a voice came to him and said, "what are you doing here Elijah?'*

14 *So he said, "I have been very zealous for the Lord God of hosts; because the children of Israel have forsaken Your covenant, torn down Your altars, and killed Your prophets with the sword. I alone am left; and they seek to take my life."*

15 *Then the Lord said to him: "Go, return on your way to the Wilderness of Damascus; and when you arrive, anoint Hazel as king over Syria.*

I have heard many testimonies of believers who have heard the still small voice of God. Some have shared with me that they have heard what they believed to have been the voice of God calling their names or have spoken messages to their spirit that they did not respond to. Later they experienced unexpected dilemmas that if they had listened to the voice they would have been better prepared to handle the unsuspected problem or could have avoided them altogether.

Others would sometimes say, "something told me to do this or that." Have you ever said that? My response to them is usually, "Who do you think that something is?" God often speaks to us in the still small voice of the Holy Spirit, yet many people still call Him "something." Remember God is not a something; He is a someone, who is alive, powerful, loving, and communicates daily with His children.

Allow God to communicate to you the way He chooses. Listen and learn to know His voice. The next time you hear what you believe to be the voice of God speaking to you, whether it is audible, a voice in your thoughts (mind), or in your spirit (heart), answer Him in reverence, humility and faith. It is the work of the Holy Spirit to speak to us as He leads and guides us in ministry.

Seek to grow in your personal fellowship with the Holy Spirit that you might know His voice. He often communicates in ways that we do not always immediately understand. The Scripture says in Isaiah 55:8 that God's thoughts are not our thoughts, neither are our ways God's ways. God can and will communicate to us in ways needful to Him to help us grow in our faith and enable us to fulfill our purposes. Whenever God speaks to us, the spiritual principle of His directions can be found in the Bible.

No. 2 — We May Ask God in Prayer

"Trust in the Lord with all your heart, And lean not on your own understanding; In all your ways acknowledge Him, And He shall direct your paths." — *Proverbs 3:5-6*

Another way of knowing your purpose is to ask God what is His purpose for your life. Sometimes God may reveal your purpose to you right away, while at other times it may require fasting and praying. In either case, it is vitally important to wait on the Lord and expect a response from Him.

God may be speaking to you right now, but to hear and receive Him your faith and attention must be at a level where you are open to hear Him. The Lord works in many different ways; therefore, when we ask him for guidance we must be vigilant yet humble in our spirits as we look and listen for his response.

Saul, who later became Paul, asked our Lord what He wanted him to do. As Saul was on his way to Damascus to persecute Christians, the scripture says in Acts 9:3-7, *"...and suddenly a light shone around him from heaven. And he fell to the ground, and heard a voice*

SEEKING DIVINE GUIDANCE

saying to him. "Saul, Saul, why are you persecuting Me?" And he said, 'Who are You, Lord?' And the Lord said, 'I am Jesus, whom you are persecuting. It is hard for you to kick against the goads.' And he trembling and astonished, said, 'Lord, what do You want me to do?' And the Lord said to him, 'Arise and go into the city, and you will be told what you must do.' And the men who journeyed with him stood speechless, hearing a voice but seeing no one."

Christ wants us to know our purposes, but when we ask Him to reveal it to us we must allow Him to answer and or reveal it in His time and His way. We must also be willing to make ourselves available for whatever and wherever God may lead us. His response may not be what we want to hear, but it will always be what is best for our lives and the kingdom of God.

When God first told me that he was going to give me a ministry to the world, I immediately started visualizing a popular TV ministry, reaching thousands of people all over the world with money flowing into the ministry. But later when God revealed to me the type of ministry He wanted me to have, it was just the opposite of the luxurious ministry I first visualized. I was disillusioned because my vision of ministry was influenced by prideful ambition. Initially I was disappointed, but God helped me to understand what Christian ministry is all about. He also helped me to understand that the gospel is not based on fame and material riches. I now feel honored and blessed to be used by God in any area of ministry that pleases Him.

When my sister-in-law, Evangelist Moore, is anointed in the spirit and begins to pray for me in prophecy, she speaks to the type of people the Lord told me He wanted me to minister to: the people of the streets, those desiring greater understanding of the scriptures, the elderly, truck drivers, runaways, drug addicts and others to whom Christ will send me. I am now ready to decrease that Christ might increase in me. Christ is emptying me of self-weaknesses that he might fill me with Himself, that I through Him might achieve the purpose he has ordained me to serve.

No. 3 — Gifts of the Holy Spirit

"Each one should use whatever gift he has received to serve others, faithfully administering God's grace in its various forms." — *I Peter 4:10 NIV*

Spiritual gift(s) are supernatural powers given to believers by the Holy Spirit to help us fulfill our God-given purposes and to exercise our roles in ministry. Wayne E. Caldwell says in his book, *The Fruit and Gifts of the Holy Spirit*, that Spiritual gifts can be classified into two categories, 1) Leadership or Enabling gifts and 2) Serving gifts for all believers. [1]

Gifts Support Our God-Given Purposes

Romans 12:4-8 tells us that believers in the body of Christ have different functions and different gifts to support our purpose in ministry according to God's will and grace for our lives.

Romans 12:4-8

4 *For as we have many members in one body, and all the members do not have the same function,*

5 *so we, being many, are one body in Christ, and every one members of one another.*

6 *Having then gifts differing according to the grace that is given to us, let us use them: if prophecy, let us prophesy in proportion to our faith;*

7 *or ministry, let us use it in our ministering; or he who teaches, in teaching;*

8 *or he who exhorts, in exhortation, he who gives, with liberality; he who leads, with diligence; he who shows mercy, with cheerfulness.*

The book of Ephesians 4:11-13 gives reference to what is generally referred to as church leadership or enabling gifts. These gifts are ordained to equip church leaders' function in ministry.

Ephesians 4:11-13

11 *And He Himself gave some to be apostles, some prophets, some evangelists, and some pastors and teachers,*

12 *for the perfecting of the saints for the work of the ministry, for the edifying of the body of Christ.*

13 *Till we all come to the unity of the faith and the knowledge of the Son of God, to a perfect man, to the measure of the stature of the fullness of Christ;*

1 Corinthians 12:8-11 provides a reference to what is generally referred to as serving gifts. Any believer in the body of Christ may have any of these gifts as it pleases God. These gifts are given to provide supernatural powers to help church leaders and laity (church members) alike serve God and man in our God-given purposes.

1 Corinthians 12:8-11

8 *For to one is given the word of wisdom by the Spirit, to another the word of knowledge by the same Spirit,*

9 *To another faith by the same Spirit, to another gifts of healings by the same Spirit,*

10 *To another the working of miracles, to another prophesy, to another discerning of spirits, to another different kinds of tongues, to another the interpretation of tongues.*

11 *But one and the same Spirit works all these things, dividing to each one individually as He wills.*

GIFTS OF THE HOLY SPIRIT

Gifts of the Holy Spirit are given to every believer to minister to both Christian and non-Christian communities. God has given us spiritual gifts that every care of the human experience can be affected in supernatural ways to His glory. All of the gifts are in the Holy Spirit, who is in us, and He will manifest each gift (supernatural ability) through us as He wills. The Holy Spirit has manifested most of these gifts in me at different times in my ministry.

A Brief definition of the Service Gifts

Wisdom: Supernatural abilities to make anointed decisions based on knowledge and understanding revealed by God.

Knowledge: A spiritual knowing — to know certain mysteries without reading it or being told by man, but by the Holy Spirit.

Faith: The supernatural ability to believe God regardless of circumstances. The substance of things hoped for, the evidence of things not seen (Heb. 11:1). Abraham had the gift of faith that demonstrated God's purpose for his life.

Healings: The Spirit of God working through a person to heal sicknesses and diseases.

Miracles: The power of God working through a believer to make supernatural things happen that bring glory to God.

Prophesy: Prophesy means to foretell and to speak

the words of God. In either case the message should come from God.

Discerning of Spirits: The supernatural ability to identify different spirits or types of spirits that come into one's presence.

Different kinds of tongues: The supernatural ability to speak in a heavenly language interpreted only by and through the Holy Spirit.

Interpretation of tongues: The supernatural ability to interpret what has been spoken in tongues.

Using Our Gifts in the World

To get the most out of our Christian witness, we must use our gifts in non-Christian communities as well as in Christian communities, as led by the Holy Spirit. However, the gift(s) may be operated and administered differently as it pleases God. I am the business administrator for the church I attend, and my work is primarily administrative in my secular occupation. I was hired in that position because of my administrative abilities (a spiritual gift as referenced in 1 Corinthians 12:28) and, by the grace of God, I continue to be successful in that area. I shared this information as an example of how gifts can be used in Christian as well as non-Christian communities. I know that God is the source of my abilities, and I give Him the glory for it.

While engaged in my secular work, as I have opportunity, I put the spiritual principles of scripture into practice by encouraging fellow employees to live on the job and at home to the glory of God. I try to never stop doing my secular work to teach the Bible. However, every now and then when I run into someone who is not ashamed to talk about the goodness of God, it gives me joy to remind them that the "Lord is still good." Or when I get an anointing in my spirit, I have to raise my hands and say, "Thank you, Jesus."

In our secular work each of us as believers should make a conscious effort to live our faith to the glory of God, and as we have opportunity encourage other believers to remember that their help comes from God as well. When the situation presents itself, we should also inform non-believers that there is a greater power watching over us who cares and can fix any problem we may have. Our lives should be lived daily in demonstration of God's love so that others might know God's love through us and are encouraged to live their lives to the glory of God.

Allow the Spirit to Control Your Gifts

As you recognize and accept your gift(s), allow the Holy Spirit to be in control. The Spirit knows the mind of Christ, ow He wants to minister, and to what degree He wants His supernatural power to contribute in our victories. There are some things Christ has given us the power to do, and He wants us to do it with the authority and directions He has given us. In other things, Christ wants us to do our part as He does His part. Still there are things Christ wants to do for us all by Himself, without our intervention. When we allow the Spirit to be in control, He will lead us in our degree of participation in each ministry activity.

Trust Christ's will, directions, and power to bring about positive results in your ministry service. As He operates in your ministry, do not expect Him to administer His gifts in you the same way He administers His gifts through others. We cannot control the results of the Spirit's power working in our ministries, but we can influence the outcomes by our faith and obedience to God's will.

Gifts Are Manifested In Different Ways

In 1981 my wife's aunt was diagnosed with cancer, I didn't know it at the time but she was dying. I knew that 'she had been going back and forth to the doctor and in and out of the hospital. None of her medicines seemed to have been doing her much good and I felt helpless. At that time I was a Sunday School teacher and had just recently accepted my calling as a preacher of the gospel. I had taught many Sunday school lessons on divine healing, how Christ healed many that were sick during the New Testament period. I also taught His promises that He is able and will heal us today. I had a passionate desire to take Christ at His word to heal my wife's aunt.

One Sunday after morning worship services, I asked my wife to go with me to her aunt's house to pray with her, asking the Father, in Jesus' name, to heal her sick body. I said to myself, "I'm teaching every Sunday morning that God will heal and deliver us from our sickness and diseases, if we pray and ask him in faith. Now I'm going to my wife's aunt's house, and I am going to pray as sincerely and fervently as I know how that God would heal her." I was looking for an immediate response from God.

When we arrived at my wife's aunt's house, she was sitting in a chair with her hands in her lap. After saying our greetings and having a small chat, I asked her if we could pray with her, she agreed. I led the prayer; I prayed until my eyes were full with tears and my face began to sweat. I prayed until I had nothing else to ask God.

After I stopped praying and began to wipe the sweat from my face, I noticed our aunt raising her left arm and hand up into the air toward the ceiling and back toward her lap again several times. I didn't know what was happening, but she began to smile and say, "Thank you, Jesus." I thought she was just raising her arm giving praises to the Lord because of the prayer. But then she told us that prior to the prayer she could not use her left arm and hand at all. After witnessing such a miraculous event my spirit leaped within me with joy and confidence, now knowing for myself that God, Jehovah-Rophe, "is the God who heals."

Christ has since used me in ministry to bring about healing in the lives of many within our congregation. I don't always see immediate manifestation of healings to everyone I pray with, but the Holy Spirit fulfills Christ's promises to heal each individual as He wills through our individual ministries.

No. 4 — Visions and Dreams

"And it will come to pass in the last days, says God, I will pour out of My Spirit on all Flesh; And your sons and your daughters will prophesy, And your young men will see visions, And your old men will dream dreams. – Acts 2:17

Christ may reveal our purpose through dreams and visions. The angel of God spoke to Joseph who was betroth to Mary, the Mother of Jesus, in a dream by night giving him guidance on God's plan for his role in the incarnate birth.

Matthew 1: 20-21
20 *But while he thought about these things, behold, an angel of the Lord appeared to him in a dream,*

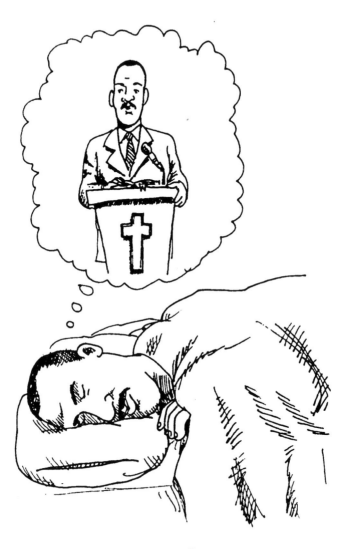

VISIONS AND DREAMS

saying, "Joseph, son of David, do not be afraid to take to you Mary your wife, for that which is conceived in her is of the Holy Spirit.

21 *"And she will bring forth a Son, and you shall call His name Jesus, for He will save His people from their sins."*

Throughout the New Testament period Jesus Christ has spoken to his servants in dreams and visions. Dreams and visions have been given for but not limited to:
- Prophecy
- Knowledge
- Guidance
- Warnings
- Instructions

The Lord spoke to the Apostle Peter in a vision while he was in a trance in the city of Joppa (Acts 10:9-23). In the vision the Lord prepared Peter for his ministry mission to the gentiles. Peter followed Christ's guidance, and because of his obedience to the vision, the Spirit through Peter brought great glory to the Kingdom of God.

The Apostle Paul was given a vision by night while he was on his missionary journey. In the vision a man of Macedonia stood and pleaded with him saying, *"Come over to Macedonia and help us."* After he had seen the vision the Bible says in the words of Paul:

"... immediately we sought to go to Macedonia, concluding that the Lord had called us to preach the gospel to them."   Acts 16:9-10

My Personal Witness to Dreams and Visions

God has often given me ministry revelations and guidance through dreams and visions. While asleep on the night of October 3, 1998, the Lord came to me in a dream. I saw His face clearly, but could not identify his face with any particular race or color. The best I could describe Him is that He looked as if he was a mixture of all races and colors in one. He was dressed in a white robe and had a telephone book in His hands. He told me that He wanted me to tell people everywhere that each person has a God-given purpose for their existence and that each of us need Jesus Christ to help us fulfill our purpose. For my clarification, I repeated Christ's instructions back to Him to ensure that I understood Him completely. I said, "You are saying that each of us has a purpose for living and that each of us needs Jesus Christ to help us fulfill our purpose?" In the dream Christ nodded His head and said, "Yes." He told me that He wanted me to go into the teaching ministry, but he instructed me not to do anything until He told me to. Christ also told me in the dream that He was not giving me any money to start the ministry, but that I should take up as much offering as I could to help support the mission financially. This book is a step toward fulfilling the mission Christ has given me in ministry with His message to the world.

God still speaks to man through dreams and visions. The Bible says God is the same yesterday, today, and forever. Believe that Christ can and will speak to you in dreams and visions to serve his purpose. Our Christian walk is a walk of faith; do not limit the power of God to communicate to you in unique ways that glorify him.

No. 5 – Spiritual Will or Desire

"For it is God who works in you both to <u>will</u> and to <u>do</u> for His good pleasure." — Philippians 2:13

God may put a will or deep desire in our hearts to serve Him in a special way. Along with the will He gives us the ability and spiritual power to perform the work. The will or desire that God places within us to serve Him is a spiritual seed that takes root in the soils of our souls and grows up in Jesus to full bloom. And when the time is right, the seed will manifest itself according to God's purpose, at God's appointed time and or special circumstances in our lives.

I recently met a young college woman who believed in her heart that it is God's will for her, in Christian service, to become a nurse. I later thought about the difference in an individual wanting to become a nurse for economic gain versus following God's will to be in min-

A SPIRITUAL WILL TO FOLLOW GOD'S PURPOSE

istry as a nurse. I recall in the month of October 2001 I had the opportunity to meet a nurse at a local hospital who served her patient in the Spirit of Christ. As I watched her minister to her patient, I could see the love of Jesus radiating through her service. I had never seen a nurse who served with such love and compassion. She would rub the patient's arms, forehead and hair. She would get close to the patient and talk to her in a loving, caring, soft and gentle voice, just as if she were caring for her own mother. To me, she worked as if she was working, as the Scripture says, *"as unto the Lord."* A friend sitting beside me observed the nurse at work and said to me, "I was in this hospital a month ago and she was my nurse and she treated me the same way."

I was so amazed with the nurse as she ministered to the patient that I said to her, "You seem to really care about your patients and appear to love your work." She replied, "I do, I love my work, and I try to care for each patient as if I am caring for my own mother."

It appeared to me that she had a spiritual anointing upon her nursing skills. I was blessed by just watching her care for her patient with such love. The work did not appear to be a job for her, but a ministry.

When God puts a will or spirit within an individual to serve His purpose, obedience to God should always have first priority in the individual's life. The financial and material rewards that follow are benefits. Never allow the desire to achieve financial and material success to take priority over your will to serve God's purpose, in His time and in His way. The scripture says in Matthew 6:33: *"Seek ye first the Kingdom of God and His righ-teousness, and all these things will be added to you."*

Early Preparation

God may start preparing us for our ministry purpose at an early age. At the age of 10, not very long after giving my life to Jesus Christ, a spiritual will came into my heart that I could not control to become a preacher. I remember living in South Carolina, as a little boy, about two-tenths of a mile from a cousin's house where I spent a lot of time doing what most children do. I can recall many days while walking from my cousin's house I would preach all the way home, as long as no one was watching. As I grew through different stages of my life, the will to preach would never go away. During my teen years, I confessed that I did many of the foolish things some teenagers do, but still deep within my spirit the will to be a preacher lingered.

During my military days, away from family and friends, I spent a lot of my time on weekends in night clubs, trying to party away the will to be a preacher. I wanted to continue to be a Christian, but I did not want the responsibility nor the commitment of preaching. I tried using profanity for a few weeks, something I had never done before. I was spiritually convicted, and the desire to preach kept coming back.

Many times God places individuals in our lives to encourage us to move in the direction of our God chosen purpose. I remember being at a friend's house one evening when an out-of-town pastor was visiting. I did not know the pastor nor did he know me. But after a short conversation with him, the pastor said to me, "Son, I can see that you grew up in a Christian home. Do you still go to Church?"

My response was, "No, sir." I still had the courtesy of saying yes and no sir or ma'am to adults.

When he ended the conversation, he said, "Son, I can see something in you (he was referring to a spiritual anointing) and I'm asking you to go back to church. I'm not going to ask you to stop living the way you are living; I'm just asking you to go back to church."

Those words weighed heavily in my spirit; I remember them as if it were yesterday. After my honorable discharge from the United States Air Force I started going back to church and renewed my faith in Jesus Christ.

I remember on several occasions believers anointed with the gift of prophecy would say to me, "You are going to be a preacher." Most of the time I would get angry, smile or laugh it off, and in my mind I would say in denial, "They don't know what they are talking about."

I remember meeting my wife's former pastor, whom I did not know very well, in a local shopping center. He asked me if I had started preaching yet. I now regrettably responded with sarcasm and said, "Who said I was going to preach?"

His only reply was, "You are going to preach." He smiled and walked away.

Even though I expressed anger in my response to the pastor, yet deep down within my heart I knew that God's will that lingered within my spirit for years was to be. The scripture says in Philippians 2:13: *"For it is God who works in you both to will and to do for His good pleasure."*

Surrendering to the Call of God

One Sunday night in the month of October 1981, after a full day of worship, I was lying in bed dozing off to sleep. But instead of going to sleep, I was taken into a spiritual trance. I was not asleep, but at the same time I was not fully awake. I had no control over what was going on. In the trance I saw myself standing at the fork of two long, dark, lonesome roads. At the end of the road on the left there was complete darkness. The road on the right was also long, dark and lonesome, but at the end of the road I could see a distant, small, bright light. My body began to shake and tremble all over, like a leaf of a tree blown in a turbulent windstorm. The Spirit of God moved with power within me and caused me to consciously get up out of my bed and kneel humbly before the altar in our living room. That deep spiritual will within me that had lingered for years suddenly manifested itself within me with power and confidence and moved me to say, "Yes, Lord, I'll do your will, I'll preach your gospel."

Just as I spoke those words, I felt the Spirit of God pouring out His anointing upon me like I had never experienced it before. It felt like a 55-gallon barrel of cold rainwater pouring all over me from the top of my head flowing to every part of my body. I began to praise and glorify God right there in our living room with all my might. And yet, it was not my might but the power of the Spirit of God manifesting Himself within me.

No. 6 - Frequent Opportunities to Serve

"Furthermore, when I came to Troas to preach Christ's gospel, and a door was opened to me by the Lord."　　　　　*— 2 Cor. 2:12*

In this method God uses frequent opportunities for us to serve Him in special ways that reveal or prepare us to serve His purpose. When we exercise those opportunities they often bring us spiritual fulfillment, inner joy, and/or agreement in and with the Spirit of God. Obeying our God-called purpose is not always pleasant or mountain-top experiences. Sometimes following God's directions for our lives can become a spiritual

FREQUENT DOOR OF OPPORTUNITY

and physical struggle. But Christ has promised never to leave us nor forsake us. Therefore, whatever the cost, let us pray that we yield our lives to his trusting and powerful hands.

David's Frequent Opportunities to Serve

David, a commander in King Saul's army, was given many opportunities to lead Israel into military battles. God was with him and blessed him to be a valiant military leader. The Lord worked so mightily in David as a military leader that as they were returning home from battle the women would sing and dance in the streets saying, *"Saul killed his thousands and David killed his ten thousands."* 1 Samuel 18:6-7.

God used those military leadership opportunities to prepare David for a greater task that He had planned for David's life. David would one day become King of Israel.

Opportunities When You Feel Least Of All

God can use us in His service even when we feel like the least of all. The manifestation of our individual ministry purpose may be revealed during different stages, circumstances, and spiritual levels in our walk with Christ.

I have a brother who because of illness had to quit his career job in the air conditioning repair business prior to retirement age. His illness has grown to the extent that he has to go to the hospital for medical treatment one to three days every week. I try to call him every weekend to give him spiritual encouragement. Some weeks when I call and ask him how he is feeling he sounds spiritually uplifted; however, at other times he confesses his faith and seems to just be holding on.

During a telephone conversation in the month of December of 2001, he said to me, "I don't know what the Lord is keeping me here (alive) for, but I believe He is keeping me here for some reason." I asked him if he had any idea what God wants him to do; his response was "no." He said that he couldn't do anything for God now that he was sick and couldn't get around very much at all.

I began telling him how blessed he was to be a father, grandfather and great-grandfather. How he still has a good mind to think and recall events of his life. How he could teach spiritual truths to his children and grandchildren and affect their lives in positive ways. I stated that through his positive influences on his children and grandchildren it might prepare them to touch the lives of hundreds of other people in positive ways.

Just then he interrupted and said, "All I do is kiss the elderly women when I go to the hospital and make them smile." Suddenly an anointing chill overshadowed my spirit that said, "That's it, Christ many times gives us opportunities in ministry at different phases and circumstances of our lives."

I responded to my brother, "Maybe your purpose in ministry during this phase of your life is to bring a smile to the sick and elderly." I shared that thought to let him know that Christ can and will use anyone in ministry if they would allow Him to. I continued, "I do believe that if we could help others smile or laugh during their adversities it will many times give them enough strength to face their adversities with less fear and discouragement. And while you are making those sick and elderly women smile, let the love of Christ radiate your presence." The Psalmist says, *"The joy of the Lord is your strength."* — Nehemiah 8:10.

Sometimes the little things that seem so insignificant can be God's way of fulfilling His purpose through us. The love of God made visible through our service for Christ can also serve others in a smile.

No. 7 – Talents and Natural Abilities Anointed for Ministry

" For who makes you differ from another? And what do you have that you did not receive?…"
1 Corinthians 4:7

All abilities whether they are natural (called talents) or spiritual (called gifts) are given by God. God created

all men for His glory. Therefore, God can change each of us to the person He wants us to be.

Talents and Natural Abilities

Talents and natural abilities are given at our birth and are developed as we grow through life. The Holy Spirit may use our various talents and abilities for God's purpose as it pleases Him. But in addition, He also bestows spiritual gifts after a person is born again. This is illustrated in the life of the Apostle Paul. Before his conversion he was a talented leader and persuader of men. But his gifts of healings, miracles and apostle-ship were not given him until after his conversion. [1]

Barbers and Beauticians in Ministry

Christian ministry can occur in most law-abiding professions; however, the believer must be a servant of Christ. I have an acquaintance who is a beautician whose skills have been anointed by God for ministry. She is an amazing person with a beautiful personality. She loves God, she loves people and she loves hair.

During a conversation with her at her place of employment, as she was caring for my daughter's hair, she told me that she prays for every client and every client's hair. She stated that every client's hair that she cares for grows over a period of time to be healthier and longer.

As she spoke to me, she was smiling as if caring for her client's hair gave her spiritual fulfillment. She said, "This is my Ministry."

My barber spends her evenings and days off going to nursing homes and homes of sick and shut-in clients, giving free hair cuts to those who could not afford it. She confesses that this is God's purpose for her in *ministry* at this point in her life.

Musicians in Ministry

I have seen musicians with natural abilities to play musical instruments receive Jesus Christ into their lives and became greater musicians for the Lord. The Holy Spirit has anointed their various abilities and is using them mightily to the glory of God. Many have great singing ministries for Jesus Christ in the local church worship as well as one-on-one ministries. Some have become church leaders: evangelists, pastors, priests, prophets, teachers, and powerful saints in the work of the Lord.

Health Care Workers in Ministry

God needs ministers in the health care field. I have seen and heard of nurses who have given their lives to Christ became anointed in the Spirit, and in addition to their secular jobs used their abilities for the kingdom of

God in ministering free services to the sick of their communities. They help the elderly take their medicines on time and see that their doctors' appointments are made and kept.

I'm also associated with a Home Health Care worker anointed in the love of God giving free time to those in need of home health care support.

I have known of doctors forming alliances to give free medical attention to people without medical insurance or financial support.

I am also acquainted with a dentist well established in his practice who has gone back to college to grow in biblical studies to become better equipped to do whatever God has for him to do in Christian service.

Builders in Ministry

God needs builders in ministry, born again building contractors and volunteer workers led in the Spirit to form work groups to fix up the houses of the poor and needy. God need contractors to oversee church building programs at home and abroad. They can also be utilized to give free professional advice and supplies and labor to young couples and others low on the poverty scales to build or remodel their houses.

Athletes in Ministry

I have read about major league sports players who have committed their lives and have become faithful ministers of Christ. They live lives of holiness on and off the courts and/or fields. They are positive Christian role models to thousands of young children, teenagers, and adults alike. They have given and continue to give hundreds of thousands of dollars to various communities and other charitable causes.

Farmers in Ministry

God needs farmers to go into foreign and under-developed countries to teach foreign farmers how to irrigate and cultivate the land, and to fertilize their crops for proper growth. Teaching them how to increase their crop yields by proper use of pesticides and modern farming techniques to get the most out of their growing seasons. There are many thousands of people starving from hunger in all parts of the world, even in this great country of ours (the United States of America). Christian ministers are needed everywhere. I can now better understand the great commission of going into "all the world."

Endless Possibilities

Imagine lawyers willing to be attorneys for the Kingdom of God by taking the cases of the poor and financially distressed. Lawmakers, local and national, standing up for Christ in upholding Christian values and the love of God in their law-making decisions. Judges taking a stand for Jesus by ensuring that their decisions are just and fair, upholding the brotherhood of man and the lordship of Jesus Christ. Think of trash collectors anointed in the Spirit spending selected weekends picking up the trash of the elderly and those less fortunate.

Imagine accountants anointed in the Spirit giving free home budgeting, financial and tax planning services to those who cannot afford a professional accountant or consultant. Businessmen anointed for ministry can be used in various ways for the Kingdom of God. The ministry is always in need of finances to support the great commission to reach the whole world for Jesus Christ. Christ can and will take talents, skills and natural abilities and use them for the glory of God.

Ministering to the Children

One of the greatest needs of our time is for mothers, fathers, siblings, teachers, positive role models, community workers and Christian believers to minister to the growing needs of young people in our communities and throughout the world.

I believe that most young people are self-respecting, are growing up in godly and/or wholesome family environments, and have dreams and desires that they are trying to achieve. However, there are a growing number of children involved in drugs, crimes, gangs and underage and out-of-wedlock sexual behaviors. Many lack respect for authorities, respect for the rights and properties of others, and even their own lives.

Christ needs and is equipping workers to reach out in love to encourage, train and direct young people to become healthy, productive, and spiritually wholesome individuals. God also need ministers to reach the babies and toddlers, to teach them wholesome Christian values at an early age. Do you enjoy or are you gifted to work with young people? Are you available to the Kingdom for Christian service? Finally, are you willing to be molded by Christ to serve His purpose?

The opportunities to minister in the Kingdom of God on earth in this present age are endless. Remember the words of our Saviour, *"Go ye into all the world."*

Ministering to the Whole Person

While serving in your anointed talent, skill or natural ability, the Holy Spirit may also want to manifest His supernatural powers through you as you serve others.

There are people in every walk of life who need to be ministered to, physically, emotionally, financially, and spiritually. As God uses you to help bring emotional healing to someone's life, He may also want to use you supernaturally through the gifts of the Holy Spirit to heal that person's sick body. As God uses you to help a person financially, He may also want you to speak to them supernaturally, under the anointing of the Holy Spirit, in a word of prophecy. God may want to work a miracle through you for someone who is without shelter or is hurting in some way.

Do you have a talent, skill or natural ability that can be used to the glory of God? Is the Holy Spirit stirring your mind and heart to use your talents, skills, or abilities for the good of the Kingdom of God? Remember that ministry is serving the needs of man in the power of the Spirit in the name of Jesus Christ our Lord.

3

Preparation for Service Is A Process

"To everything there is a season, a time for every purpose under heaven."   — *Ecclesiastes 3:1*

Our ministry callings are revealed at different times and spiritual levels in our walk with Jesus Christ. To some people, like the prophet Amos, God may speak and send them forth to do His work immediately. To some, like John the Baptist and the Apostle Paul, Christ may take through a period of preparation, to build them up spiritually, before he sends them forth to do His service. Other people, like myself, Christ had to empty (bring me down) of self to fill me (build me up) with Himself in preparation for the journey. Only Jesus Christ can prepare us for His service; the scripture says our righteous acts are like filthy rags. Therefore, without Jesus Christ we can do nothing.

Our Steps Are Directed By God

Since October 1998, when Christ initially spoke to

me concerning His will to change my ministry service, He has spoken to me on several occasions instructing me on steps to take in ministry that neither others nor I understood. I am reminded of the words of God through the Prophet Isaiah 55:8, *"For My thoughts are not your thoughts, nor are your ways My ways,' says the Lord."*

In September of 1999, Christ spoke to me and told me to step down from being the moderator of a mainstream denomination church association. In May of 2000 while in prayer in my office prior to the Sunday morning worship, the lord spoke to me and told me that my work was over at the church where I, at the time, served as pastor. Initially I did not understand. Can you imagine God telling you that your work was over? I thought He was about to take me home to Glory. I reverently and humbly asked God if he was taking me home to Glory. His response was "no." I was very relieved with that response. It is my desire to live out God's purpose for my life on earth before I'm called home to Glory. He told me not to step down from the office of pastor until He gave me further instructions.

God can and will give us step-by-step directions in serving our purpose. In September of 2000, the Lord spoke to me again and told me to give up my pastoral position. I noticed that every step the Lord gave me seems to have been stepping down from a position of honor, at least in the eyes of man. Each time the Lord spoke to me and gave me instructions in ministry He also gave me the discipline and strength to obey Him.

Three months before the Lord told me to step down from pastoring, a fellow pastor called me from Dallas, Texas, early one Sunday morning, in March of 2000, as I was preparing for Sunday school. He gave me a word of prophecy from the Lord. He told me that the Lord told him to call and tell me that my ministry would decrease and my wife's ministry would increase. He said the Lord told him to tell me not to worry, because God has a purpose and a plan for what He is doing in me. He said, " God is bringing you down that God Himself might raise you up." Again those actions confirmed the scriptures in Philippians 2:13 that says, ***"For it is God who works in you both to will and to do for His good pleasure."***

Since that time the Holy Spirit has often given me spiritual revelations and teachings on ways to know and live our God-given purposes.

Emptying of Self

In order for some of us to allow Christ to work in us like He wants to, we have to be emptied of ourselves that Christ might work freely and mightily in us. To be emptied is to be purged of the passions and desires of the flesh. It is a spiritual cleansing.

Many of us want to be fully surrendered to Christ for His purpose and glory. However, within us are certain ways, habits, beliefs, values, thought patterns, and behaviors that are not pleasing to God. And God, who is holy, desires us to be holy in every area of our conduct. *"... as obedient children, not conforming yourselves to the former lust, as in your ignorance; but as He who has called you is holy, you also be holy in all your conduct"* (1 Peter 1 :14-15).

Those areas of our lives that have not matured in holiness give God the least glory. God cannot use some of our ways in the work He has prepared for us. God can get the most out of our lives and is more richly glorified when we're holy in every ounce of our being.

God has brought many of us a long way in our spiritual growth and development. However, some of us are not where we would like to be or where God wants us to be spiritually. Some of our weaknesses we are aware of, other weaknesses many of us cannot readily see or identify with, but we know we have them. That is one reason it is so important to trust God even when we don't know what is going on in our lives. He works on our known as well as our unknown weaknesses and develops our strengths in ways we cannot always understand. So, when we are being purged and don't know why we are being purged, just let God have His way.

Christ wants to purge our fleshly nature that He might fill us with Himself. Ephesians 4:22-24 says, *"that you put off, concerning your former conduct, the old man which is corrupt according to the deceitful lusts, and be renewed in the spirit of your mind, and that you put on the new man which was created according to God, in righteousness and true holiness."*

While Christ is working on us He is also working for our good. Christ wants us to crucify the flesh with its passions and desires. As we are being emptied of fleshly desires Christ is filling us with His character, evidenced through the fruits and gifts of the Holy Spirit.

4

Making It Personal And Applicable

*"Wisdom is supreme; therefore get wisdom.
Though it cost all you have, get understanding."*
                                        –Proverbs. 4:7

At this point you may be anxious to find out more specifically how to know God's purpose for your life. Although only the Spirit of God can answer this question for you, I will attempt to lead you through a process of hearing Jesus Christ as he reveals your purpose to you, through ways we have previously discussed.

Reflect on your Past

Look back over your life, your entire life, as far back as you can remember. Follow the paths of your life and try to remember how God may have been leading, equipping or working in your life as it relates to the service of God and the betterment of mankind? Reflect on situations, events, activities, opportunities, talents, skills, natural abilities, spiritual gifts, visions and dreams, spiritual wills or desires, times when you may have asked God about your purpose or times when the voice of God may have spoken to you. Think of times you may have helped others, unaware that you may have been preparing for service in God's purpose for your life. Draw from these and other situations in your life to get a better under- standing of how God may have been revealing your pur- pose to you.

Sharpen Your Focus

What area(s) of service to God and man seemed to have been the focus of your life, even if you did not use those opportunities to bring direct glorify to God? Ask God to reveal to you if certain events of your life were preparatory stages for future opportunities in ministry. Have you found yourself frequently helping others in physical, emotional, financial or spiritual ways? Most importantly, did your paths allow you to help others see the love of Jesus Christ, even though your intent may have been an act of goodwill?

Making It Applicable to You By Faith

What or where is your area of passion as it relates to the ways God used you to help others? Is it an area that allows you to help others for their good and the good of the Kingdom of God, unselfishly? Is there a spiritual drawing or leading in your heart? Does it bring glory to God?

Is there an agreement in your spirit, even though it may not be what your mind wants to do? Have you prayed for God's guidance? Is there a specific area you believe by faith that God is leading you in ministry? Do you believe in your heart that this is God's will for your life?

If the answer to these questions is "no" or "I'm not certain," then continue to draw closer to God in faith and holiness, prayer, study and worship. Develop a stronger personal fellowship with Jesus Christ in your daily living. Make Jesus your best friend. Ask Him for His purpose for your life and look to Him with expectation to receive your answer. If the need arises fast and pray, earnestly seeking God's will. Our lives will be much more fulfilled and blessed when we are living the purpose for which we are called.

"All things work together for good to those who love the lord and are called according to His purpose for them."

(Roman 8:28 New Living Translation)

If the answer to these questions is "yes," then act on what you believe is your purpose by faith. In the words of Apostle Paul in his second epistle to the church at Corinth, *"We walk by faith and not by sight."* (2 Cor. 5:7)

Acknowledge God and by faith follow what you believe God is leading you to do. Speak with your pastor or spiritual advisor for spiritual support and ways your ministry can be of help to the local church. Again the scripture says in Proverbs 3:5-6:

> *"Trust in the Lord with all your heart and lean not on your own understanding, in all your ways acknowledge Him and he shall direct your path."*

As you step forward in the direction you believe by faith God is leading you, always remain flexible and available to his guidance. As He grows us, taking us from glory to glory in our purpose, He may also change our course, all to His glory.

What Lets Us Know When We Are On Track With God's Purpose for Our lives?

I believe that there should be evidences in every believer's life that let them know if they are on track with God's will for their lives. When we are not on track with God's purpose for our lives, we may often have a feeling of incompleteness, emptiness, a thirst for something more, lack of direction, and a feeling of not being spiritually fulfilled.

Outside Of God's Purpose For Your Life

> ➢ Emptiness
> ➢ Lack of Fulfillment
> ➢ Thirst For Something More

On Track with God's Purpose for Your Life

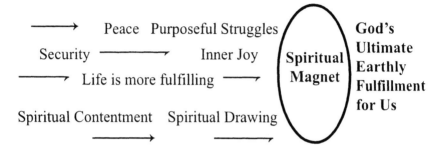

Peace   Purposeful Struggles

Security ———→   Inner Joy

———→ Life is more fulfilling ———→

Spiritual Contentment   Spiritual Drawing

Spiritual Magnet

God's Ultimate Earthly Fulfillment for Us

Outside of God's Purpose For Your Life

> ➢ Feeling of being off track
> ➢ Lack of direction
> ➢ Self controlling inner spirit

When we are on track with God's purpose for our lives, it may be revealed to us in different ways. Some have expressed having a spiritual peace, contentment, and inner joy. Others have expressed a sense of divine security and comfort. I continually experience spiritual fulfillment, inner joy, and an inspirational drawing that is pulling me, in love, in the direction of my God-given mission.

5

Step Out In Faith – Remembering Who Called You

"....For if I still pleased men, I would not be a servant of Christ." — *Galatians 1:10*

As you step out by faith in your God-given purpose, it is not uncommon for fear to arise. Ask God to remove all doubts and dreadful fears from your mind and heart as you seek to move forward in His service. Whatever work Christ has for you he will be with you, protect you, empower you, and lead you to a victorious finish.

2 Timothy 1:7 says:

7 *God has not given us the spirit of fear, but of power, love and of a sound mind.*

There is a healthy fear and a harmful fear. Healthy fear responds in reverence or respect, harmful fear responds in terror or dread.[2] Four reasons for harmful fear come to mind: fear of failure, fear of persecution, fear of rejection, and fear of pain. Our love for and confidence in Christ should grow to be of more value to us than the things we fear. A willingness to endure suffering for the sake of Christ pleases God. The scripture says, *" For it is better, if it is the will of God, to suffer for doing good than for doing evil."* 1 Peter 3:17

Do not be alarmed if your ministry purpose is not administered or operated the same way other ministries are. God has given each of us different strengths, gifts, personalities, and abilities that he may use in different ways as it pleases Him. He does not expect us to minister like anyone else. God intentionally made each of us unique.

There is such an abundance of depth, height, and breadth in God that every ministry can operate at a different level and be successful in Him. Therefore, we should not compare ourselves to other ministries as a measure of our successes in the work of the Kingdom. In fact, comparing ourselves among ourselves is contrary to the word of God. Our successes are in the hands of Christ, again influenced by our faith and obedience.

The question is, are we doing individually what Christ has told us to do? Our individual obedience has an interconnecting effect upon the whole body of Jesus Christ universally.

Our Lord wants each of us to listen to the Holy Spirit and let Him equip and guide us as to how He wants to use us for His glory. Failing to listen to the Spirit of Christ can result in us doing what we want to do or what we think we should be doing for Christ rather than doing what Christ has purposed us to do. In the final day of accountability, each of us must give an account of our service according to Christ's will for our lives.

Your Claim to Your Purpose May Be Challenged

While many people will embrace your calling and encourage you onward, there will be others who will doubt your calling and reject your Christian fellowship. Regardless of man's rejections, hold on to what Christ has given you to do, always remember who called you. Christ calls us to our ministry purposes according to His will and purpose, not according to the opinion of men.

The book of Hebrews 5:1 tells us that God calls men from among men and appoints them to things pertaining to God. The scripture also says in 1 Corinthians 2:11b *"... Even so no one knows the things of God except the Spirit of God."*

So when the Spirit of Christ reveals your calling to you, follow Him when and wherever He leads. Men doubted the ministry calling of the Apostle Paul. Many people doubted the person and ministry of Jesus Christ Himself. So, if men doubt your calling, remember that you are identifying with the suffering of Jesus Christ.

In 1990 when my wife and I were led by the Spirit of God to leave the first church I pastored in El Dorado, Kansas, to plant a new church in Wichita, Kansas, other church leaders called me crazy. They did not understand the diverse operation of God, neither did I. Some said that I had no church building, no congregation, and no salary to go to. I don't always understand how or why God does things the way He does while He is doing it; I just believe Him, trust Him, and obey Him. I knew without a doubt that I was following God's directions for my life.

In 1999 when the Spirit of Christ told me to step down from the seemingly prestigious position of moderator of a mainstream denomination, again other church leaders nor I understood what God was doing. Although I did not understand, Christ gave me the commitment and obedience to do what He directed me to do.

Again in 1999 when the Spirit of God told me to leave a mainstream denomination for the work He had for me to do, about fifteen of twenty-two churches that we previously fellowshipped with stopped fellow-shipping with our church. But God had already warned me of it before it happened. The ministry of Jesus Christ is not limited to denominations; the gospel is a ministry to the world. We were determined to please God, even though it meant losing Christian fellowships. I'm not going to tell you that following God's instructions was always easy, but God gave us the will and the strength to obey Him, even when it was unpopular among men.

It was also in 1999 when Christ told me that He wanted to use my wife in ministry. After I licensed her to preach, three more of the remaining seven churches stopped fellow-shipping with us. Through all that we endured we were determined to follow the will of God for our lives.

In the year 2000 when God told me to step down from pastoring and told my wife to take up the office of pastor, two of the remaining four churches discontinued their fellowship with us.

As we grow to a deeper relationship with God and seek to be fully surrendered in following the will of Jesus Christ for our lives, many people will not understand us. The Spirit of Christ will strengthen us to serve even when it is humiliating and unpopular among men. As I have read in the scriptures, Christ endured the shame for us all.

Even though following Christ's directions presented many challenges to us, I still find peace and inner joy through it all. God continues to bless our lives and supplies our family and church congregation with abundance.

During every step Christ led us through, He kept a scripture in my heart that weighs heavily in my spirit that says, "...*For if I still pleased men, I would not be a servant of Christ*" – Galatians 1:10. Regardless of the persecution we would endure, my wife and I are committed to obeying the voice of Christ above the voice of man. Our relationships with Jesus are personal; we are sold out for Him.

While many believers questioned our obedience to Christ, I'm so thankful that there were other believers encouraging us to go forward in Jesus. There are many Christians who do not limit the power and sovereignty of God to use us in ministry as he will.

The Great Need for Ministers

Christ wants to use each of us in unusual ways. The ways of man are not the ways of God. Do you know anyone in any of the following categories who needs to be ministered to? Are you gifted to minister to them spiritually? Do you have a natural ability anointed for God's service to help them? They may be in your neighborhood, right next door, in another continent or even in your own home.

The intent of the great commission given to man by Christ is to reach people in every area of society. Many will not come to the local church seeking a life in Jesus Christ, although we all need Him. Therefore, Christ has commissioned us, the church, through our individual callings, to go to the world and lead men to Him. We are members of the body of Christ called to serve in different roles in the work of the kingdom.

Romans 12:4-5
4 *For as we have many members in one body, and all the members do not have the same function,*
5 *so we, being many, are one body in Christ, and every one members of one another.*

Areas of Ministry – Partial List

➤ The Unsaved
➤ Struggling Saints
➤ Hurting Individuals
➤ Fatherless Children
➤ Widows
➤ Orphans
➤ Motherless Children
➤ The Dying
➤ Demon-possessed
 and/or oppressed
➤ Elderly People
➤ Weak People
➤ Sick People
➤ Jobless People
➤ Hungry People
➤ Homeless People
➤ Those without Utilities
➤ Dysfunctional Families
➤ Pimps
➤ Prostitutes
➤ Persons in emotional
 bondage

➤ Gamblers
➤ Liars
➤ Alcoholics
➤ Bereaved
➤ Drug Addicts
➤ Thieves
➤ Runaways
➤ The Uneducated
➤ Gangsters
➤ Sex Offenders
➤ Prisoners
➤ Racists
➤ The Misguided
➤ Murderers
➤ The Selfish Rich
➤ The Proud and Lofty
➤ Those needing help
 and encouragement
➤ Those needing to hear
 from God
➤ Those in bondage to
 ungodly habits

Walking By Faith

Christ wants us to trust Him and follow His guidance in ministry even when we don't know where we
are going. After resigning from the church in El Dorado,

Kansas in August 1990, God opened the door for us to continue His ministry purpose for us within two months. In October of 1990, my wife and I signed a contract to purchase an existing church building on the west side of Wichita, with no church members nor salary. The church building was complete with pulpit and altar furnishings, pews with hymn books and bibles, a piano, a kitchen equipped with appliances, classroom tables and chairs, a pastor's study fully equipped with desk, chairs, bibles, and a library of about 250 reference and Christian helps books.

The building was purchased, rededicated, and ready for worship, the only thing needed was people. On the very same night of our closing on the church building, a young mother came to our home with three young children and asked us if we would start a Bible study with her family. She had no idea that we had just closed on a church building. The following night six of us had Bible study in our new church building. The experience with that young mother and her family was no coincidence, it was the hands of God at work in our ministry. What a mighty God we serve! When we obey God He makes ways for us.

During the first few years at our newly planted church there were times when the church funds were low and we needed money to pay church and vehicle insurance. God never forsook us. The church would often receive hundreds of dollars through the mail, or God would send someone by who would put hundreds of dollars in the offering tray just when we needed it.

From the day of our first Bible study to this day, twelve years later, my wife and I have not had to pay one church bill out of our household funds; Christ always provided. Again, while some believers encouraged us, other believers persecuted us for our acts of faith. But Christ always proved and continues to prove Himself faithful to his purpose working in us. Many souls have come to Christ or have renewed their faith in Christ through our obedience to our God-called ministries.

Persecutions come along with obeying Christ. As we are used by God to bring people out of darkness to His marvelous light, remember that many will come from Satan's territory. Satan will not sit idle, he will fight back. Ephesians 6:12 says, *"For we do not wrestle against flesh and blood, but against principalities, against powers, against the rulers of the darkness of this age, against spiritual wickedness in the heavenly places."*

Never be afraid to follow God's will for your life. Remember, God is omniscient, omnipresent and omnipotent; the world and everything in it is under God's power and authority. Therefore, as we serve Christ we are in His divine care and protection. Also remember, *"...we are more than conquerors through Him who loved us."* Romans 8:37.

The work of the flesh is to bring fear and distrust into our relationship with Christ. Humbly take authority over your fleshly desires, in the Spirit, and stand on the Word to overcome your fears.

Sometimes as we deny our fleshly desires we will hurt or even suffer, but be assured that God will never leave nor forsake us. We are who Christ says we are, and we can do what Christ says we can do, and we can be whatever Christ says we can be. The Apostle Paul said to the Philippians (Phil. 4:13): ***"I can do all things through Christ who strengthens me."***

6

Ministering in the Holy Spirit

"But as it is written: 'Eye has not seen nor ear heard, Nor have entered into the heart of man The things which God has prepared for those who love Him.' But God has revealed them to us by His Spirit. For the Spirit searches all things, yes, the deep things of God." — *1 Cor. 2:9-10*

The Holy Spirit, the divine Spirit of God, lives within the heart of every believer. He is God manifesting Himself in Spirit. He speaks to us and provides ways, opportunities, and power to carry out God's will. You and I need more than our natural wisdom and understanding to understand the things of God, because the things of God are spiritually discerned. The Holy Spirit knows and receives from the mind and will of the Father and brings directions to each believer's life. As believers, we need both the teachings of the Scriptures and daily fellowship in the Spirit of God to get the most out of our faith. The Bible helps us to know God, to know our relationship to God, and what God expects of us through

His Son Jesus Christ. The scripture says in Psalms 119:105: *"Your Word is a lamp to my feet and a light for my path."*

The Holy Spirit makes the word of God personal, guides us in its applicability, tells us how and when to use the Word and gives us power both in our *general* and *individual* ministries to obey the Word. The scripture says in 1 Corinthians 2:11b-12, *"Even so no one knows the things of God except the Spirit of God. Now we have received, not the spirit of the world, but the Spirit who is from God, that we might know the things that have been freely given to us by God."*

The Holy Spirit can and will guide us, in times of need, even when we are not knowledgeable of the Word. Our challenge is our ability to hear and know His guidance. It is hard to hear the voice of the Holy Spirit if we are emotionally upset, tired or busy with this world's agenda. Sit down, be quiet, meditate, and go to your secret place and commune with God. Listen and be watchful as the Spirit of God speaks to your heart and acts upon the will of God for your life in ministry.

The flesh, the old nature, is constantly tempting us to fulfill our personal desires apart from the will of God. If we walk in the Spirit of God, we will not obey the desires of the flesh.

"So I advise you to live according to your new life in the Holy Spirit. Then you won't be doing what your sinful nature craves. The old sinful nature loves to do

evil, which is just opposite from what the Holy Spirit wants. And the Spirit gives us desires that are opposite from what the sinful nature desires. These two forces are constantly fighting each other, and your choices are never free from this conflict..." (Galatians 5:16-17, New Living Translation).

It is vitally important that as believers we have a conscious living fellowship with the Spirit of God as we live our purpose. Having fellowship in the Spirit blesses us to know and feel the presence of God's love, joy, assurance, confidence, and security as He leads us from glory to glory, from one spiritual level to another.

7

Live Your Purpose to the Glory of God

This last chapter will be used to allow the words of God to speak to you directly. In each of the following passages the scriptures are speaking directly to us, giving biblical guidance as we live our ministries to the glory of God. The Apostle Paul writes to the saints at Ephesus and Rome encouraging them to fulfill their God given purpose to serve. As you and I now know, we can only fulfill our purpose in and through Jesus Christ. Read this chapter daily as you begin believing and living your call to service by faith:

Ephesians 4: 1-3 (New Living Translation)
Therefore I, a prisoner for serving the Lord, beg you to lead a life worthy of your calling, for you have been called by God. Be humble and gentle. Be patient with each other, making allowance for each other's faults because of your love. Always keep yourselves united in the Holy Spirit, and bind yourselves together with peace.

Romans 12:6-11 (New Living Translation)

God has given each of us the ability to do cer-
tain things well. So if God has given you the
ability to prophesy, speak out when you have
faith that God is speaking through you. If your
gift is that of serving others, serve them well. If
you are a teacher, do a good job of teaching, If
your gift is to encourage others, do it! If you
have money, share it generously. If God has
given you leadership ability, take the responsi-
bility seriously. And if you have a gift for show-
ing kindness to others, do it gladly.

Don't just pretend that you love others. Re-
ally love them. Hate what is wrong. Stand on
the side of the good. Love each other with genu-
ine affection, and take delight in honoring each
other. Never be lazy in your work, but serve the
Lord enthusiastically."

Finally, I will end this chapter and book with the
promise of God to those who live in obedience to His
will in ministry:

Matt. 25:34-40 (The New King James Bible)

34   *"Then the King will say to those on His right hand,*
     'Come, you blessed of My Father, inherit the king-
     dom prepared for you from the foundation of the
     world:

35 *'for I was hungry and you gave Me food; I was thirsty and you gave Me drink; I was a stranger and you took Me in;*

36 *'I was naked and you clothed me; I was sick and you visited Me; I was in prison and you came to Me.'*

37 *"Then the righteous will answer Him saying, 'Lord, when did we see You hungry and feed You, or thirsty and give You drink?*

38 *'When did we see You a stranger and take You in, or naked and clothe You?*

39 *"Or when did we see You sick, or in prison, and come to see You?'*

40 *"And the King will answer and say to them, 'Assuredly, I say to you, inasmuch as you have done it to one of the least of these My brethren, you have done it to Me.'*

Enjoy the Journey

NOTES

[1] Wayne E. Caldwell

[2] Ronald F. Youngblood, New Illustrated Bible
   Dictionary, 1995

BIBLIOGRAPHY

The Ryrie Study Bible, King James Version, (Moody Press – Chicago),
Copright 1985

The New King James Bible, New Testament, (Thomas Nelson Publishers – Nashville – Camden – New York). Copyright 1979

The NIV Study Bible, New International Version, (Zondervan Publishing House – Grand Rapid, MI 43520, USA), Copyright 1995

Wayne E. Caldwell, the Fruit And Gifts of the Holy Spirit, (The Wesley
Press – Marion, Indiana), Copyright 1979

R. F. Youngblood, F. F. Bruce & R. K. Harrison, New Illustrated Bible
Dictionary, (Nelson – Nashville –Atlanta –London – Vancouver), Copyright 1995